ISLANDS OF THE GULF

To fellow New Zealanders and overseas visitors, welcome to the Hauraki Gulf and the natural splendour of this magnificent waterway, with its many islands and attractions.

Please respect nature and its beauty by leaving it unpolluted, so we may pass this national asset on to our future generations for them to enjoy.

ISLANDS OF THE GULF

PHOTOGRAPHS
David Kerr

TEXT
Kirsten Warner

Hodder Moa Beckett

Acknowledgements

A very special thanks to Alex, Hamish and my wife Annie, for the patience and understanding when I was away on location the many times over the long hot summer.

I would like to thank the many who have helped me with this photographic journey, including Skyferry, The Nature First Group, Adventure and Nature Cruises, Safari Tours, Heletranz and Kawau Kat.

Thanks also to Mike & Dee and master bird photographer Geoff Moon, aboard the *Te Aroha*, in tandem with the Department of Conservation, for access to Little Barrier Island. — *David Kerr*

As an Aucklander living on the inner Waitemata Harbour at Meola Reef, the Hauraki Gulf is an indelible part of my life and my family's. Writing about the Gulf has reawakened my desire to further explore this wonderful seascape. My heartfelt thanks to Bernard Griffen for sharing his experiences as a mariner and his contribution to the writing of the book. — *Kirsten Warner*

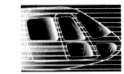
Helicopter adventure charters at their best!

SKYFERRY

"Safari Tours for Great Barrier Island Adventures"

Proudly Serving Kawau Island & The Gulf

THE NATURE FIRST GROUP
Proudly supporting conservation in New Zealand

Cover and half title page: Oneroa Beach, Waiheke Island
Title page: Rangitoto Island

ISBN 1-86958-211-X

© Hodder Moa Beckett Publishers Limited   © Photographs David Kerr   DOSLI Map Licence PL098898/5

Published in 1995 by Hodder Moa Beckett Publishers Limited, [a member of the Hodder Headline Group]
28 Poland Road, Glenfield, Auckland, New Zealand,

Printed through Colorcraft, Hong Kong

All rights reserved. No part of this publication may be reproduced or transmitted in any form or by any means, electronic or mechanical, including photocopying, recording, or any information storage and retrieval system, without permission in writing from the publisher.

On a still day, the islands of the Hauraki Gulf float on an endless, shimmering plate of ocean the way a child floats daisies on a saucer of water. Pictured here, Motutapere Island and Whanganui Island settle in front of the Coromandel Harbour.

INTRODUCTION

IMAGINE you could take to the air like the extinct New Zealand eagle and soar high above the great expanse of water enclosing the romantic islands of the Hauraki Gulf. Using the currents of air you climb up above the dark circle of Rangitoto Island and its perfect central cone and across Waiheke Island and the necklace of smaller islands.

You can see the magic mountain range called Moehau forming the backbone of the Coromandel Peninsula and holding the southern boundary of the Gulf. From your bird's-eye point of view, it looks as if great dark Moehau makes up the body of a south seas Loch Ness monster, a taniwha whose tail loops under the water and emerges again as the mountainous Aotea or Great Barrier Island.

The great tail dips deep down under the sea and up again at Hauturu or Little Barrier Island, its last spines again pricking the surface of the ocean as the Hen and Chickens group of islands off Bream Head.

From Bream Head to Cape Colville, these outer islands form the northern perimeter of the Hauraki Gulf, the glorious stretch of water which is one of the great scenic beauties of New Zealand.

Seen from high above, the Firth of Thames separates Coromandel from the Auckland coast like a giant thumb print filled with shallow water. From there, the mainland coast up to Bream Head at the mouth of the Whangarei Harbour is laced by waterways, harbours and small peninsulas. At Auckland city, the Waitemata Harbour encroaches so far into the North Island it nearly dissects it and meets the Manukau Harbour and another ocean.

Within these land and island borders, there are more than 40 islands scattered across the Hauraki Gulf. Their countless beaches, bays and coves provide endless diversion and entertainment for Aucklanders at play.

Aucklanders love the water. They build houses by it, they swim in it, they join clubs associated with it, they build lifestyles around it, they base property values on views of it. Their activities involving the sea are increasingly diverse, and largely centre on the Hauraki Gulf.

For generations, the stepping off point to idyllic days exploring the magical blue waters of the Gulf has been the gateway of the downtown ferry terminus. The curves and graces of the historic Ferry Building, framed by the stark facade of a modern high rise, is a reminder of the Gulf's rich history.

Inspired by experts who believe conservation is a human activity and not something that takes place in isolation, many Aucklanders have enthusiastically embraced the Hauraki Gulf's protection, flocking to annual rubbish clean ups and planting days at island reforestation projects such as Tiritiri Matangi Island. Here, an island has been replanted, serving as a model for other islands.

Not surprisingly, the Auckland region has the highest level of boat ownership in the country. It is estimated that nearly 30 per cent of Aucklanders participate in boating of one kind or another – from dinghys, waka, kayaks, canoes, wind surfs and yachts to surf skis, launches, power boats travelling at increasingly high speeds and luxury cruisers. Some of the greatest yachties in the world started out in baby-sized P-class yachts here.

Swimmers compete to cross the Gulf. And parties of novice kayakers under the guidance of Olympic gold medallist Ian Ferguson regularly leave the shelter of Okahu Bay on the waterfront to paddle to Rangitoto and climb to the peak in time for sunset across the city.

Children grow up sailing as soon as, or even before, they can walk. Mid-week, Aucklanders are racing on the Gulf. Weekends from Friday night, the marinas are emptying with a steady stream of craft under motor and sail heading out to the Gulf. Ferries constantly cross and recross the familiar waterways, connecting island residents to the mainland and taking a flow, and in summer a flood, of passengers out to this marine playground.

From our earliest years, we New Zealanders recognise the chant of the radio weather forecaster, warning of rising south-westerlies "from Bream Head to Cape Colville". It has an evocative, nostalgic charm to it, that phrase, beckoning us out to adventure and to the sea. That sea is the Hauraki Gulf, entered at the first of the string of lights from Bream Head, past the big light at Coppermine Island, then Cape Rodney, down to Flat Rock and the rising loom of Tiritiri Matangi and Rangitoto, guiding shipping along the marine pathway to Auckland.

Fast craft, like seagulls floating head to the wind, alongside a harbour leading light buoy. They buzz around the Gulf carrying keen leisure fishermen to catch snapper, kingfish and kahawai at their favourite spots.

This lovely stretch of over 7450 square kilometres of South Pacific Ocean is home to a wonderful diversity of activities and habitats, from the port of Auckland and the nation's naval base at Devonport, to important fishing grounds, historic buildings, a marine reserve, an internationally protected wetland and wildlife sanctuaries of world importance. The Hauraki Gulf has been inhabited for so long there is no island or piece of coastline which does not have a precious historic site.

The last moments of island life go too quickly as the ferry comes into sight at Tryphena Harbour.

The progress across the Hauraki Gulf of New Zealand's early Governor, Sir George Grey, can be traced by the exotic trees he collected and introduced. Phoenix palms guard one of the gentle, sheltered harbours of Kawau Island, once owned by Grey as a place of retreat from political life.

It seems that everyone's Gulf is a different Gulf. For divers, it is the underwater paradise of the outer islands and the marine reserve at Goat Island near Leigh. They say that because of run-off from the land, the water is too cloudy at the inner islands for diving.

For yachties, there is a certain superiority in their intimate knowledge of the remoter islands. They have their favourite spots, their nautical language, tales of foul weather and fair cruising, and they get all edgy if they haven't been out sailing for two weeks.

Oneroa Beach, Waiheke Island. Sitting in the sun on a quiet beach is an idyllic way to enjoy the Gulf.

Windsurfers have their own tracks and haunts, enjoying the sudden squalls and quick changes of weather so characteristic of this water. Fishermen tramp the channels en route to commercial grounds, reading the lights and markers like motorists read road signs, alert to the constant traffic of tugs, barges, pilot boats, ferries and big ships bound for the port of Auckland.

And then there are non-nautical folk whose lives are influenced too by the Gulf's mood changes, and shaped by experiences of the Gulf – crossing the Harbour Bridge, for example, or sitting on Takapuna Beach lulled by the lapping of water, the passage of shipping in the channel and the presence of Rangitoto just off the beach, forever adolescent and moody.

The islands offer inspiration to nature lovers, amateur geologists, botanists, bird watchers, painters, photographers, hikers and people merely seeking solitude.

They go camping, they enjoy bird-watching or observing marine life on the foreshores, they walk the island forests and scenic coastal tracks, they go hunting in remote parts of the bigger islands, they dive, fish, ride horses and bikes and idle away brilliant days on the beautiful beaches of the Hauraki Gulf.

The islands themselves are distinctly different in character, geography and in size. For many people, Great Barrier Island is the most special, and they talk about it as a mystical and spiritual place. For others, spreading and gentle Waiheke, with its Mediterranean climate, epitomises the charm and ambience of the Gulf.

Undoubtedly, though, it is the Gulf's youngest and closest island, Rangitoto, which is the symbol and central landmark of Auckland, the heart of both the City of Sails and the Gulf.

Wherever you are in the Gulf and Auckland, Rangitoto looms like a giant's kneecap. You can see why Maori described the skyline as the three knuckles of a local chief called Peretu – "Nga Pona toru a Peretu".

Rangitoto's perfect volcanic cone, the bump of North Head and double bumps of Browns (Motukorea) Island are part of a system of volcanic crests and craters peculiar to Auckland's landscape and character.

No one lives permanently on Rangitoto Island, and as you approach it, the last few remaining baches on the

The seemingly unspoiled raw appeal of Rangitoto Island is in fact carefully monitored and maintained by the Department of Conservation. In the 1920s and 1930s convict labourers built the salt water swimming pool, paths and roads on the island.

There is a lot of nostalgia for the glorious days of the *Baroona* and the double deck, twin-nosed steam and coal-fired ferries which rolled and heaved their way through the Gulf's moods to Waiheke and Devonport. But if you ask old-timers how they prefer to travel, they'll tell you on one of the fast ferries, according to the skipper.

Rangitoto is the most curious place. Its equivalent landscape would be one of the active volcanic islands southern shore seem as oddly placed as dolls' houses, smaller than matchboxes under the shelter of the mountain. The new vegetation beginning to cover the island has a rich, boucle texture like dark olive-green astrakhan.

Fields of lava spill like black porridge with a light sprinkling of grey lichen sugaring the top. The raw patches look like mounds of truffles, bulbous, textured, porous and bare of vegetation. But slowly the island is beginning the process of creating forest.

The only sign of life on a slow winter's morning is two parked Department of Conservation utes. "It's all go on the island today," comments the dry-as-a-bone skipper of the Fuller's ferry as he noses into the single strand of wooden wharf. Fuller's glide a fleet of jet-propelled ferries around the Hauraki Gulf which have virtually replaced the old wooden boats.

in Hawaii or the Philippines. There is silence, deep silence, if you stop on one of the paths built by convict labour with pick, shovel and wheelbarrow in the 1920s. Apart from the scrunch of footsteps on gravel, there is only an occasional bird call.

Recent scientific estimates date the island at around 650 years old. The drama of an island spewing itself out of the ocean is vividly recorded in the oral history of Maori who lived on and cultivated the surrounding islands. Witnesses of other eruptions say the approach of molten lava sounds like shattering glass.

In fact, the island gave birth to itself right on the doorstep of Motutapu, showering that island's gardens with ash, which Motutapu gardeners mixed with sand to fertilise the land. Footprints have been found in successive layers of ash on Motutapu, which indicate Maori villagers returned between dustings.

From Rangitoto, you can clearly see the terracing covering most of Motutapu, shaping today's bare pasture like waves of hair across a head. It's obvious from the scale of the earthworks just how big a population this horticulture supported. Probably thousands of people once lived here in the dozen or so pa or villages which have been located along with over 300 historic Maori sites.

The Arawa and Tainui canoes arrived at Rangitoto in the 14th century. One version of the name Rangitoto is traced back to the day the commanders of the two canoes quarrelled and fought and the island's full name Te Rangi i Totongia a Tamatekapua means "the day that the blood of Tamatekapua was shed".

More commonly the Maori origin of Rangitoto is quoted as meaning "bleeding sky" relating to the blood red sky of its eruption.

Nothing moves on Rangitoto except tourists toiling their way up the hour's walk to the summit. There are very few birds, because there is no surface water. Rainwater drains rapidly away, captured in a lens of fresh water inside the island. In summer the black rock retains heat and becomes scorching hot.

Occasionally you pass rugged motorbikes parked at the side of the road belonging to Department of Conservation staff and hunters who pursue the last remaining opossums and wallaby with ruthless intensity.

The city of Auckland seems just a stone's throw away from Rangitoto's summit, and the city's hum is audible. The Gulf seems to go on forever. Here is the closest you'll get to the mighty New Zealand eagle's eye view.

Built directly onto stone, some of Rangitoto's baches are bright and quirky, with neat shell paths and gardens of succulents; others are damp and decaying.

Below, the narrow channel separating Motutapu and Rangitoto, now crossed by causeway, is a deep milky green. The channel has silted up in the past 170 years, but it still seems ludicrous that opinionated and wilful missionary Reverend Samuel Marsden ever insisted on sailing around this side of Rangitoto. Of course he got stuck.

You can imagine how comical it looked to Maori watching his antics from island vantage points. And how small those sailing vessels were. Fifty men were able to haul the boat into deeper water.

From Rangitoto, the Gulf spreads out like a great dinner plate. Container ships waiting in the Rangitoto Channel are dwarfed like bath toys. To the north, the folds of Whangaparaoa and Mahurangi enfold Kawau Island. Tiritiri Matangi Island sits like a pincushion, Little Barrier Island is, as usual, wreathed in mist, and 90 kilometres away to the east Great Barrier Island and Coromandel finish the circle.

From here you can see the Gulf as an entity in itself made up of the sky above, the land underneath and the water. Within it, the contrasts are rich and diverse – from the estuarine Firth of Thames, breeding ground for tens of thousands of wading birds which set off every year on epic migrations to the Arctic and subarctic, to the rocky Mokohinau Islands where muttonbirds are traditionally gathered for food by Maori.

Wherever you are in the Hauraki Gulf, the pohutukawa with its gnarled and trailing root system clings to the most inhospitable cliffs, trailing its branches over secluded bays, and wreathing the shoreline in glorious scarlet blossom just before Christmas. In some places the pohutukawa, sensitive to the invasion of picnickers boiling their billies among its roots and the ravages of opossums, stands alone. In other more protected places we can see veritable forests of this giant of the landscape.

Rangitoto Light is to Auckland what the Statue of Liberty is to New York. It sits like a piece of candy rock or a barber's pole on the reef at the south-west tip of the island, welcoming visitors and locals to the channel and the ports of Auckland.

The Auckland Department of Conservation says the historical significance of the Hauraki Gulf is, in general, very much underappreciated. The Gulf is rich in both Maori and Pakeha history and in many ways it's a boating history. For almost 1000 years these marine pathways have been constantly travelled, first by Maori craft then later by sailing ships, schooners, scows, steamships, yachts, freighters and cruisers.

When the first European explorers arrived in New Zealand, they found Polynesian navigators had beaten them to it by hundreds of years. Pacific voyagers arrived perhaps 800 years ago and settled in coastal regions. Such early sites of population are found at Motutapu, Great Barrier and Browns Islands. In those days there were moa and seal to be caught in the islands and water of the Gulf.

As the population grew, agriculture was increasingly important for food supplies and settlement was influenced by the location of fertile and friable land. Volcanic soil, found on the path of the lava flows from the Tamaki Isthmus' numerous volcanoes, was fertile and easy to work. And the cones were good defensive sites for fortifications.

Originally Hauraki was the name given to the settlement where Thames stands today. Waitemata was originally spelt Wai Te Maata, or "the waters of Te Maata". The Maori call the Gulf as a whole Tikapa, using their name for Gannet Rock off the north-east coast of Waiheke, a place which was sacred for historical reasons.

In 1642, Abel Tasman had landed on the west coast of the South Island but sailed nowhere near the Hauraki Gulf. For 117 years the islands of New Zealand were unvisited by white-faced foreigners, until the arrival of Captain Cook in late spring 1769. Cook and his scientists observed the transit of Mercury on the eastern side of Coromandel and then rounded Cape Colville at the tip of the Coromandel Peninsula.

For a week Cook sailed up the Hauraki coast of Coromandel naming the string of islands at the mouth of the Coromandel Harbour the Eastward Isles (Whanganui Island today). He named the southern reaches of the Gulf the Firth of Thames and noted there was a large settlement at the mouth of the Waihou River.

Because of strong south-westerly winds, Cook ventured no further into the Gulf than Ponui and Waiheke Islands and as he sailed on northwards, he called the two large islands enclosing this large expanse of water Great and Little Barrier. He named Cape Rodney and Bream Head as he passed but missed Whangarei Harbour because of bad weather.

The pock-marked volcanic face of Browns Island, which erupted about 20,000 years ago, is a favourite landmark for Aucklanders, lying only 1.6 kilometres from the mainland. Submerged lava-flows off the coast warn boaties of hidden dangers just beneath the surface. It has been cleared for several hundred years and was farmed for nearly 150 years. Like almost all the other islands of the Gulf, it is of outstanding historical importance.

It was the beginning of contact with Europe. When the poor and rowdy of England were dropped at the penal colony of New South Wales, traders made their way across the Tasman Sea looking for timber and flax. Whalers, sealers and missionaries arrived, and the first recorded voyage of a white man into the Waitemata Harbour was by Reverend Samuel Marsden in the early 1820s.

Not long afterwards the French explorer Dumond D'Urville entered the inner Gulf, leaving his name by way of the D'Urville Rocks north of Waiheke Island.

The name Hauraki means "Winds From the North" and with the winds came war. In 1820, the Ngapuhi chief Hongi Hika visited England with missionary Thomas Kendall and returned with muskets and powder. His incursions laid waste to the populous region of the Hauraki Gulf.

There was some attempt at European settlement of

the Gulf in the mid-1820s when Waiheke Island was bought from Maori. But Ngapuhi raiders struck fear into the hearts of isolated and vulnerable European settlers and they moved on.

They left behind infections which proved even more fatal to Maori than the musket, and the ravages of disease further decimated the Maori population.

In 1841 the capital of New Zealand shifted from the Bay of Islands to Auckland and settlers bought or took up disused Maori land. Large parts of all the islands of the Gulf were bought and settled quickly.

The Gulf provided timber, and much of the building of the new capital was done with shingle from Waiheke Island, which also ran a brisk trade in firewood and charcoal. Mineral deposits were found on several islands, and there was a short-lived gold rush on Great Barrier Island.

The strong, straight and tall kauri, in forests which covered all of the mainland and most of the islands, provided the raw material for a timber boom. Where there was kauri, there was also the golden kauri gum.

Milling continued on Great Barrier Island until the early 1940s, longer than on most places on the mainland. In its heyday the bustling timber mill village at Whangaparapara on Great Barrier supported more than 300 people.

Once the timber was taken out, the land was cleared for farming. The rich fish life of the Gulf now helped support settler-farmers whose resources were limited to what they could eke out from the land and sea. Visits from trading ships were infrequent and money scarce.

Today it is easy to forget the hardship and isolation that was an everyday reality for those early settler families, close-knit in their immediate communities but without even the support of a doctor or nurse to attend a difficult birth or set a broken limb. The cemeteries of the gulf tell how families fared, and tell also of the sudden misfortunes wrought by storms at sea.

There were several notable shipwrecks. The worst was in 1894 when the passenger steamship Wairarapa, on her way home from Sydney in terrible weather, struck the cliffs at Miner's Head on the north-west tip of Great Barrier Island at full speed and 135 lives were lost.

The resort potential of Waiheke Island in particular was recognised early and by the time the Northern Steamship Company was formed in 1881 the colonial passion for boating and monster picnic excursions was gathering momentum.

We can only imagine the festive atmosphere as thousands of passengers disembarked from steamers at popular excursion spots like Home Bay on Motutapu, at Mansion House Bay on Kawau Island and Cowes Bay on Waiheke Island. Edwardians at play, dressed in narrow-waisted starched muslin dresses, corsets, high collars, suits and ties, carried with them lavish picnics, heavy canvas

Farming was always tough on Great Barrier, and with the decline in coastal shipping after World War II, pasture was left to revert to scrub and bush.

tents and even teapots in the sweltering summer heat and humidity.

At Home Bay, as at Governor Grey's Kawau Island retreat, a menagerie of exotic wildlife was introduced, including ostriches, emus, red deer, donkeys, and today's arch pests, the opossum and the wallaby.

Only ghosts and sketchy photographs remain of the private hotel at Cowes Bay which was once the social Mecca of the Gulf and hosted the annual Waiheke regatta. Gone too is the era of the boarding house, so popular in the Gulf until the 1930s.

The first boarding houses were built at farmsteads in the bays, where families put up tents and then built cabins and boarding wings for summer visitors. These enterprises employed everyone in the family, to run launches to and from Auckland, take guests out fishing, cook on massive wood stoves, bottle preserves from farm orchards, make butter, bread, cheese and soap, wash acres of linen boiled in coppers, grow vegetables and gather seafood.

Waiheke Island was sub-divided for residential and holiday homes and promoted as a marine suburb of Auckland from the first two decades of the century. The fastest Auckland set went baching on Waiheke, and there was a unique bach settlement at Rangitoto Island where Devonport Borough Council, which administered it for the Crown, leased sections to raise money.

Tenure on Rangitoto was later limited to the lifetime of the current leaseholder, and once that expired, sheds and baches straggling the shoreline were demolished. Many of the remaining baches today, with their corrugated iron chimneys, privies and water tanks, have received only the minimum of maintenance and no improvements since the 1930s. The Department of Conservation now wants to preserve buildings with architectural, historical or social merit.

The icons of mid-summer island life around the Four Square store at Little Oneroa, Waiheke Island – cold drinks and icecreams, bread trays, sand on bare feet, teeshirts and bathing suits, cruising in the back of the ute and a leisurely chat.

As Waiheke Island's population grew, Great Barrier's shrank. The decline of coastal shipping spelled the end of the farming boom on Great Barrier and much of the grazing land, held against encroaching bush with difficulty, was left to go to scrub. Hippies and lifestylers, attracted by the wild lawless feeling of the Barrier, bought up blocks of land. During the summer months you can hear the police helicopters buzzing overhead as they search, often unsuccessfully, for marijuana plantations.

The Hauraki Gulf is much more than an expanse of water enclosing islands. The sea itself has enormous importance, signposted by named fishing grounds, reefs and individual rocks.

The inter-connecting life of this entity we call the Gulf starts with rivers and streams flowing into it bringing nutrients which feed seasonal plant plankton at the beginning of the food chain.

The contrasts of the Gulf are captured in this photograph of yachts nestled in Matiatia Bay on Waiheke Island beneath rolling farmland. Once "bold, craggy and thickly timbered" according to missionary Samuel Marsden, by 1850 the best of Waiheke Island's kauri was milled. Today, tourism and wineries rank as important as farming to the island economy.

At Stony Batter, at the remote eastern end of Waiheke Island, the military built huge concrete gun emplacements linked by a warren of underground tunnels as part of the coastal defence network. Walking in to the site over private land takes about 90 minutes.

Some days you can see miles of birds working together. There's a frenzied thrashing of water as large schools of kahawai herd small fish to the surface; bigger kingfish, hammer-head sharks and bronze whalers chase the kahawai, and sea birds dive and fight for food. Birds roost and nest on the islands in millions, and their droppings, enriched by fish, provide nutrients for lush sub-tropical vegetation.

You can imagine what the Gulf was like when boat builder and dashing yachtsman Albert Sanford first went fishing there in 1864 and brought his delicious hot smoked snapper to sell at the wharves. Even now, long-time fishermen will tell you how big the crayfish and snapper used to be – and show fading black and white snapshots to prove it. Some fishermen will tell you they still are.

New Zealanders, blessed with a long and generous coastline, have always believed it is their right to go down to the sea to get a feed for the family. It is one of the most precious treasures of life to many New Zealanders, and near to the core of their identity.

The Hauraki Gulf is ideal for marine farming of oysters and mussels because of the generous flow of fresh water from islands and mainland. Sailing or steaming into a quiet harbour, even on a fine day, mussel racks look like a dark grid against the water, as if a farm fence has fallen into the sea and stayed upright.

The ever-changing moods of the Gulf are part of its allure and charm. For most of the year, the Hauraki Gulf is a beautiful, calm, tranquil stretch of water, cut by strong tides, especially down the side of Coromandel and where the water runs between islands in close proximity. For inexperienced mariners who believe it is all-forgiving, the sudden changes of weather can be swift and treacherous.

Within an hour, the south-westerly can go from calm to 45 knots in gusts, and that can mean an incredibly uncomfortable and rain drenched retreat from an afternoon sail or a terrifying slog down the Motuihi Channel on a Sunday night when you're due back at work the next morning.

Winds are variable, prevailing from the west or south-west, but the most damaging are from the north. Four or fives times a year, sometimes more, and usually from New Year until late February or March, tropical cyclones that sweep across from Australia to the Pacific Islands get trapped between two ridges of high pressure and are squeezed down to the north of New Zealand. The first sign of this, in glassy calm weather, is a large swell rolling from the north.

Closely following the swell are high winds and torrential rain. Only occasionally does the full force of a tropical cyclone hit the coast of New Zealand, but when it does, the Gulf is completely vulnerable and exposed to the north-east.

It's no time to be at sea for any creature. The Hauraki Gulf looks swollen and angry, and because it's so shallow the water becomes turbulent, covered in white caps, with a swell at times rising to four metres. Salt sea spray shrouds the headlands, islands, lights, reefs and landmarks, warning the mariner and pleasure boatie to stay where they are or head quickly to safety.

Once the northerly calms down the swell from the north rolls for days, making beautifully formed small waves. Surfies wax their boards and zip into their wetsuits, and surfboards appear even on docile Takapuna Beach.

The east Auckland current brings subtropical water deflected by the Northland peninsula, and there are tales of coconuts and even canoe paddles or carvings washed down from Polynesia onto the seaward beaches of Great Barrier Island.

As a little girl I spent every summer day between the salt water Parnell Baths at Judge's Bay and Okahu Bay on Auckland's waterfront. My brothers and I swam and dived, burned ourselves to a deep red, ate picnics, played sports and made friends and enemies in the space of an afternoon while our parents dozed and read books under the pohutukawas.

Always within our vision was the great dark shape of Rangitoto and the gun emplacements of North Head and we knew without being told that the Hauraki Gulf was the gateway to New Zealand.

The photographs in this book capture the contrasts, the wild and wonderful freedom and the endless romance of the Gulf. For people who know its moods and treasures the pages will evoke fond and dramatic memories. For those who have yet to discover the charms of the Gulf, these pictures will entice you to begin exploring.

Kirsten Warner

Substantial holiday houses perch like long-legged sea birds on a typically steep hillside at Rakino, a small holiday island with pockets of Department of Conservation-owned land.

The steep rocky coastline of Rakino Island, lying only two kilometres north-east of Motutapu, is typical of the Gulf where small outcrops like this one mimic the form of the main island. The straggly pine may have been introduced by New Zealand's zealous Governor, Sir George Grey, who once owned Rakino.

Great Barrier Island sleeps in the outer Gulf like a giant lizard, her tail wrapped around Port Fitzroy, a safe, deep water haven famous for its fishing grounds. In this photograph, Kaikoura Island lies under the massive flanks of the Fitzroy entrance.

On the easterly side the island is more forgiving in places. Long ridges give way to valley flats suitable for farming. Here, surfers haunt some of the most beautiful, untouched and inspiring white sand beaches in the world.

For some people, the only way to really enjoy the Gulf is by boat. Others prefer more sedentary pleasures at one of Waiheke Island's perfect white sand crescents. The natural and scenic attractions of the island were promoted since the first decade of the century for holiday makers and commuters.

Looking like a great fish surfacing in the Hauraki Gulf or Maui's lost fishhook, Motuihe is the picnic island. Generations of Auckland children remember the delicious anticipation of a slow boat ride to Motuihe for the annual school outing. Now mostly in pasture, the island has a chequered and colourful past. Motuihe was sold to Europeans in 1839, and olive trees planted there by father of Auckland Sir John Logan Campbell are still fruiting. The island has been by turn a quarantine station, a prisoner of war camp, a children's health camp, naval training base and part of the coastal defence network.

In 1982, Stonyridge Vineyard's wine grower Stephen White searched for a site that mimicked the growing conditions of Bordeaux. He found it on Waiheke Island, famous for low summer rainfall and high sunshine hours. Overlooked by an olive grove, and with roses planted Bordeaux-style at the end of each row, Stonyridge lies on poor but free draining soil only a kilometre from the sea. It is planted to yield low quantities of extremely high quality fruit, and is ranked among the top New Zealand vineyards.

Farming families settled around Waiheke Island's bays. They built holding pens and races beside the beach for loading stock onto shallow bottomed scows. Early settlers rowed out to meet regular services of the flourishing coastal steamship companies. The island became the Mecca of Auckland holiday makers who camped, stayed at boarding houses or just came for day picnics. Numerous wharves were built on the island by the steamship companies and by land-owners.

Long before young professional commuters started buying Waiheke Island real estate, artists and craftspeople were drawn to the island's unconventional lifestyle. Artist Valeska Campion's sculpture at the entrance to Waiheke Kindergarten, with its Gaudi-style curves and playful, jewel-box mirrored and mural surfaces, delights both child and adult.

Kawau Island is a popular long-weekend destination, or a first leg on the sail up the coast to Tutukaka and beyond to the Bay of Islands.

Wide and easy paths through mature pine tree forests on Kawau Island provide cool shelter from the scorching summer sun.

In a matter of days, Great Barrier's castaway island magic starts to work. You take your watch off and slow down to Barrier time. The sun seems hotter, the sky bluer, the air cleaner, the beaches bigger and the walk to get there longer.

There is nothing diminutive about Little Barrier Island. Formed by volcanic eruption one and a half million years ago, it is one of the few places which shows us what the landscape was really like before human occupation. It has been treasured and strictly guarded for over 100 years as one of the most important wildlife sanctuaries in the world.

Little Barrier Island's Maori name Hauturu is said to mean Resting Place of the Winds, and early Maori navigators thought only spirits could live in this magical place. It is a botanical paradise with species which are extinct on the mainland. No one can set foot on the island, 26 kilometres east of Leigh, without a permit.

Medieval pillars of stone guard the successive ridges climbing up to Mount Hobson, Great Barrier Island's highest peak. Because of the steep terrain, transportation around the island was difficult and settlement was parochial.

Great Barrier was inhabited for much of the past 1000 years, and it is not hard to visualise the Maori villages and fortified pa which once dotted this coastline.

Like stepping into an enchanted forest, the unearthly brilliant green lake at Kawau Island is tinted by rich underground copper deposits. By 1844 New Zealand's first real industry started at Kawau Island when the first copper mine shaft was sunk. Copper mining thrived for 11 years until the below-sea-level mines were swamped and abandoned.

The keelers of the Royal New Zealand Yacht Squadron have traditionally raced from Auckland on a Friday night to invade Kawau Island for a summer weekend of further racing and play. Every other weekend of the year, the sounds of sea and nature are broken by the slap and creak of rope and sail from yachts and power boats drawn to the island.

The silvery ribs of kanuka provide a canopy for regeneration of native bush on Little Barrier Island. The absence of a wharf discourages illegal entrants to the island who bring with them the threat of accidental or deliberate introduction of predators.
The island is not completely out of bounds though. Parties are accompanied by a Department of Conservation officer as with this inflatable landing from the Te Aroha at Te Titoki Point on the south-western end of Little Barrier. The boulder beach of Little Barrier Island is one of the most beautiful sights of the Gulf, and, although difficult, the islands' only landing place.

In its heyday, Home Bay at Motutapu hosted some of the enormous picnic excursions so adored by the Edwardians. Big steamships, decked out with flags and swagging, brass band playing, disembarked up to 5000 passengers dressed in Sunday finery for a day of eating and drinking, wrestling matches, chaperoned romancing, greasy barrel competitions and strolling (not swimming) on the shore. The homestead was an elite retreat for hunting red deer released on the island in those days of pre-conservation exoticism.

Now under motor, Te Aroha is the last of the fleet of mighty scows which once plied the Hauraki Gulf. Today she carries passengers and cargo instead of kauri logs.

Rangitoto's baches are now monuments to the passing of an era. As lifetime leases expire, baches without historic, cultural or architectural significance have been demolished.

Waiheke Island. For many, island life is a return to the simple life and its pleasures.

Great Barrier is now accessible and popular with holiday makers, although, because of its isolation, passenger services were relatively recent. In the last few decades, holiday makers began buying small sections, and from the 1970s blocks of unproductive land were sold to hippies and alternative life-stylers attracted by the Barrier's outer-worldly charm.

The advent of the fast ferry brought Great Barrier Island closer to town, but it still attracts the adventurous at heart. Once you arrive, you leave the bustle behind. There are no banks, no street lighting, and travel is at a leisurely pace. The island's hillbilly vehicles are legendary although increasingly supplemented by up-to-date hire cars and tourist buses which meet visitors at the Tryphena Wharf.

Waiheke is an island of contrasts. Most people live at the western end of the island, between the ferry wharf at Matiatia and Palm Beach. The aerial photograph of Palm Beach shows how densely populated parts of this marine suburb now are. But much of Waiheke is still quite isolated farmland.

ISLANDS OF THE GULF

The great light at Tiritiri Matangi Island is one of the earliest in New Zealand and was of great importance to the mercantile development of the nation. You can see Tiri's loom from as far north as Whangarei Heads which makes it highly evocative to seafarers. It strikes a yearning for home in the heart of the restless sailor and announces arrival at the Hauraki Gulf.

Conservationists can be justly proud of the results that joint efforts by an army of volunteers and experts have accomplished in returning an island to natural splendour. Bird life on this open sanctuary is now so profuse it is virtually a nursery for native birds who decamp to the mainland to find a branch to call their own. The birds are so unused to disturbance on Tiritiri Matangi that they seem unafraid of human visitors.

Even the main shopping centre of Waiheke Island at Oneroa has a seaside resort atmosphere. Three times a week a ferry mail run brings people from smaller islands to do their shopping here.

Dotted on rocky outcrops and tiny islands all over the Hauraki Gulf, tops powdered with white droppings like cakes with icing sugar, are the homes of the Gulf's ubiquitous gannet.

The private resort island of Pakatoa, a gem in the necklace of islands stretching along the popular cruising waterway of Waiheke Channel.

Auckland is the capital of a great yachting nation, hosting the Whitbread round-the-world giants and winner of the world's most prestigious yachting prize, the America's Cup. The Hauraki Gulf offers all a yachty could ask for – the enchantment of discovery, fair winds for racing, sudden changes in weather to keep the adrenalin flowing, secluded bays, spectacular and diverse scenery and competition.

Activity as old as history. Everywhere, humans intent on launching themselves into the water, under sail, motor or paddle.

A castaway Shoal Bay harbour marker, rope edged to prevent damage to craft, announces this story book hideaway, nestled in a profusion of flax, pohutukawa and flowers at Great Barrier Island.

There is a special colour to the water at Kawau Island, an intense green reflecting dense pine forests towering above the deep inlets and coves where yachts tuck in away from the weather. There is plenty to do on shore. For a couple of dollars you can wander through the fully restored Mansion House, have tea at the kiosk, walk through forest across the island to the disused copper mine and back around the shore at low tide.

ISLANDS OF THE GULF 63

A simple task is completed in the last grace of the sunset at Waiheke Island's Matiatia Bay.

The beautiful sandy beaches on Waiheke Island are exposed to strong northerly winds which at Onetangi Beach lift salt spray across road and houses.

In pre-European times, Great Barrier Island was swathed in hardwood forests. European settlement started in 1829 when the whalers arrived. Mining for silver, gold and copper was short lived, and the island's real wealth was in its kauri timber. Giant dams were built across rivers high in the ranges to flush the logs down to the coast where they were rafted together and floated to mills.

In a country short on ruins, the towering brick chimney of the old copper mine adds a romantic touch to the landscape at Kawau Island.

Dramatically painting the picture of a treasure island or pirate shipwreck, the four-masted sailing barque Rewa sunk as a breakwater at Moturekareka, one of the string of tiny islands lying south of Kawau.

Waiheke's warm climate lends itself to unhurried alfresco living and dining at one of the island's colourful cafes at Palm Beach.

A relic of the do-it-yourself style which characterised Waiheke Island not so long ago is the old red bus which doubles as snack bar at Matiatia Wharf. It greets the hundreds and sometimes thousands of visitors who pile on and off the fast ferry service from Auckland each day. Boaties also head for Matiatia as somewhere to refuel and take on water.

It took two years to build the 30 metre high lighthouse on Tiritiri Matangi Island, and materials had to be dragged by bullock team up the island's steep flanks to the summit. Surrounded by steep cliffs, there is only one sandy beach on the island.

A tractor meets the ferry to haul visitors and Department of Conservation guide to the steep summit of Tiritiri Matangi Island where they can inspect beautifully kept white lighthouse buildings and enjoy spectacular views.

Of all the islands of the Gulf, the big, wild and legendary Great Barrier fascinates visitors more than any other. Tryphena Harbour is the largest safe anchorage and the most populated centre of life and commerce.

Several times a year, a flotilla of craft, many under motor, will take to the Waitemata Harbour for special events, such as to welcome the giants of round-the-world yacht racing. Massed displays of craft are much enjoyed in a city of boat owners and sailors.

Many New Zealand children grow up mucking about in boats, swimming off the back deck, rowing, fishing and sailing their own little yachts.

The drive on-drive off car ferry dropping its ramp as it noses island-style between clumps of toitoi into the landing at Kennedy's Point, Waiheke Island.

As the sun sets over the giant fingers of Waiheke Island and enflames the far off crown of Rangitoto Island, it is easy to see why successive waves of settlers, from the first Polynesian voyagers to the Irish and Scots who came later, fell in love with the dramatic islands of the Hauraki Gulf.

A typical approach for the kauri scow Te Aroha *as she closes with Little Barrier Island in a stiff, cold south-westerly. She's one of the last of a breed of vessel that plied the far flung reaches of the Hauraki Gulf.*